The Brightest Rock

The Brightest Rock

POEMS BY KELLY LENOX

Word Tech Editions | 2017

Front cover and detail pp. 16–17, 46–47, 72–73:
"Marks Made Cannot Be Unmade" by Susan Skryzcki.
Acrylic and gold leaf on paper. 2016. 18 x 24 inches.
Back cover and interior photographs by the author.
pp. 4–5, 7: Eagle Creek, Columbia Gorge, Oregon
pp. 100–103 and back cover: South Fork Merced River,
Yosemite National Park

Published by WordTech Editions
P.O. Box 541106
Cincinnati, Ohio 45254–1106

ISBN: 9781625492241

Poetry Editor: Kevin Walzer
Business Editor: Lori Jareo

Visit us on the web at www.wordtechweb.com

ACKNOWLEDGMENTS

I am grateful to the following publications for publishing poems in this book, some in slightly different form.

American Journal of Nursing "Mudsick"

Cave Region Review "Voodoo Lily," "The Marriage House," "Labyrinth, New Year," "Tom's Creek Falls," "Seascape," *"One need not be a Chamber— to be Haunted—"* "The Mine Tour," "Holy Ground"

Faultline "Story"

Hubbub "Cleawox Lake"

Letters to the World (Los Angeles: Red Hen Press, 2008) "(Untitled)"

Main Street Rag "Triptych"

MARGIN "Agatha, Pin Oak," "The Cerne Giant"

pacificREVIEW "Slippery World"

poemeleon *"An Unemployed Worker's Home"*

Raven Chronicles "Crow in a Crosswalk"

RHINO "So You Want to Go Spelunking," "In the Country of the Bone Flute"

Still: The Journal "Heart of Soapstone"

Stony Thursday Book (Limerick, Ireland) "The Fullness"

Summerset Review "Travelling East," "Why I Am Not an Evangelist"

Switched-on Gutenberg "Storm Surge"

Third Wednesday "Above the Caves of Škocjan"

I am also grateful to friends, teachers, and family too numerous to name, but including my parents, Glen and Jetta Lenox, as well as Sheila Ashdown, Susan Duncan, Christine Eagon, Meredith Davies Hadaway, Anne Kayser, Barbara Korun, Chris Laskowski, Colleen McClain, David McNaron, Lauren Rusk, Liz Stevenson, Barbara Buckman Strasko, Pam Taylor, Emily Whitman, and The RiverRock Writers: Deb Akers, Melanie Green, Annie Lighthart, Paula Lowden, and Suzanne Sigafoos. The faculty and staff at Vermont College of Fine Arts showed me many doors and equipped me to walk through them, particularly Gillian Conoley, Mark Cox, Rick Jackson, the late Jack Myers, and Louise Crowley.

TABLE OF CONTENTS

1

THE FULLNESS

So what do you say when your proud, drip-nosed kid
arranges a loop of leaves and prays

it won't ever blow away? You know
snapping a photo won't keep those eyes from tears,

nor will shellac—the whole encased in a hyaline skin
becomes a thing to care about, to bend toward—

and little neighbors will toddle into your yard
each wanting one shiny, butterscotch leaf.

don't tell them that when beauty speaks
it doesn't hang around for an answer.

don't tell them about autumn at all,
about luster—the loop by this time

scattered and thinned
by cats and beetles, like any raw plan.

THE MARRIAGE HOUSE

In the yard of the house that I lived in longer
than I've ever lived anywhere, the clay
reached deeper than I could dig.

Excavation is so different from tunneling—
what you dig up is lit by the sun same as everything else.
Pale centipedes burrowing in a flurry of legs.

The spade leaves a slick wall of clay,
all of a piece, worm-halves wriggling out
like Girl Scouts from tents on a chill bright morning.

We'd layer compost and leaves,
mix and turn and plant,
but if we didn't keep at it

that clay would rise back up
and crack in the summer draught.
I always imagined we could slice it,

straight-sided like bricks,
dry them till they were hard enough
to be mortared into something useful.

That yard so small, the best use seemed to be
just to leave that clay where it lay,
impenetrable under everything we planted.

WE CALLED IT DEVIL WEED

One big serrated leaf—dark green
with white speckles on top, hairy spines underneath,
and a taproot to hell.

My husband and I think it is a flower from
the neighbor's garden; she thinks it is one of our weeds.
Once in a while, one of us will grab a spade
and upend bucketfuls of clay,
hunting each root's final taper.

Mostly we slice through it, thicker
than a finger, then fear it will sprout double.
The devil weed slowly spreads behind a small-
leafed bush whose own roots we break
with each bite of the blade.

The whole thing gets to be too much.
In November, landscapers
clear the backyard
till it's two trees, some shrubs,
and a sea of soft brown mud.

They lay out pavers, sod, mulch,
a sturdy fence. Build a deck
near the place where that bush used to grow.

January rain falls, penetrates, feeds
the new plants, feeds
what roots remain.

(UNTITLED)

Beyond the window
a garden blooms in full sun—
fly beating the glass.

VOODOO LILY

The dusky dawn
becomes a dark afternoon
heavy with the odor of voodoo lily:
its blossom of blackest crimson
and scent of rotting flesh
draw blowflies to a putrid orgy.

A tuber not many would plant,
so when it rises through the neighbor's ivy
the news spreads far and the curious come
and, fighting instinct, force their feet closer.
Not many get close enough to feel
this flower's heat.

Strange luck that it grew
on her side of the fence,
a gardener who recognized
this lily—tall as she is,
a large single petal dark as her own hair.

After that season, the ceramics
she built and fired in her basement studio
grew odder and odder until
no one bought them anymore.
When she moved, her garage sale offered

shiny purple pitchers that wouldn't pour,
bumpy leaky mugs,
speckled plates, and vases
that could hold no stem—
just the ghost of a scent.

LATE

Late in the day when no waters fall,
late in the night when no sleep comes,
late in the bone with no healing yet,
the hidden bird sings
     why me why me
in a sycamore

like the one that shaded us
after tilling the garden, half a life ago.
Our first spring in that house, we didn't know,
and minced up the tubers.
I'd never heard of sunchokes—
they sprouted everywhere.
We made meals of them.

Tonight, wind blows a train's echo closer
across this little valley.
I turn my back toward it, itching,
because even in poems
there are places you can't scratch
and I want that midnight whistle
across my shoulder blades.

The bird in the sycamore
still doesn't know
it's asking the wrong question.

OREGON OCTOBER

Today, on the birthday of one friend and the wedding
of two others, the rains have come.

We turn indoors for the first time in months
and find flowers in the fiber

of pillow covers, gauzy curtains,
the knotted rug. Fake paperwhites rise

from a dusty pot, and dried hydrangeas,
years old now, fill the vase.

Above it, firelight flickers
on a three-faced mask—

human, raven, spirit—
fringed in cedar bark.

I hear, even now, strains of banjo and fiddle
tracing hollows and secret streams...

Oh, for those long Blue Ridge mountains
rolling into the haze, for those years when belief was natural.

The white page damns me. Not for the intimacies
I've shared, but for the getting dressed afterward

and going out, asking for *Fine* and giving it freely—
such a small part of the truth.

THE CERNE GIANT

Dorset, England

Finally, the caption—*Looking up the axis*
of the giant's phallus—resolves
this photograph of white lines on grass
into the midsection of a man, his figure trenched
into a chalk hillside. At midsummer,
that axis aims straight at the rising sun.

One hand grips a raised club.
For centuries, he's been held here
by turf cutters who keep
the trench in the chalk open.
They covered him during the war
to keep bombers from reading his map.

His great mark on the land awakens a memory
of the Ring of Brodgar, far to the north.
Its huge wheel of stones inscribes the sky
over the rolling turf of its island.
They'd be matchsticks to this giant in the south.
I remember walking a path worn through the heather

within that stone circle and by halfway round,
as if drawn up by my steps, another ring rises from the moor,
surrounding me in currents of light, of song
almost heard, whirling faster, faster
than my humming bones ever could alone,
wreathing the thinness of the place

and its solid grip on my moving body.
I'd be there still, would not have broken
that circle for the world. But it slipped away
when my child called me to the car,
my family waiting for me to take my place,
and I turned, walking easily between two rocks.

At home with this book, old Orkney
still arcs and loops within me. If my feet
could trace the body of this Cerne Giant
from his ankle to his hip—
shoulder—head—down
his other side and up again...

What might arise from the chalk
on stout legs, inhabit its vast perimeter,
lift one grassy hand?

What of his life
would I carry with me,
tall as the very hill?

STORM SURGE

Piran, Slovenia

A ragged, sooty front crosses the noon sun
and in the sudden dusk, boats pitch toward their berths.
From waterfront restaurants, umbrellas take flight.
Gale-whipped to triumphant pitch, waves
explode along the harbor wall,
and I run through the edges of wind and rain,
jagged as the silhouette of the Apennines
just vanished from the western horizon.

But the lightning's already running further
from its thunder and the storm blows inland.
The breeze is cold now
and you are too far away to warm me.
I walk around the point
and find on the seawall a sponge, as pale
as my coat, ripped from the underwater rocks.
I let all the live things out of it

except for two tiny green plants, firmly rooted.
It weighs nothing. I bring it home for us,
not thinking they will die along the way.

CLEAWOX LAKE

Our arrival is at night. Mars and Venus
play badminton with the moon,
which, even as we watch, gets lost in the hedge.

Teetering over a missing porch step,
I shine the flashlight away
from what belongs underneath.

The cabin's dank air penetrates our clothing,
displaces breath. The refrigerator alone is bright,
dense with half-used condiments.

The back door's path and my map both end
at this lake among the dunes. *See p. 43.*
Page forty-three shows a different lake, its shore mismatched

like irregular plaid—the sleeve
of the tartan robe firmly attached
at the shoulder, green line askew. Only the eye

zigs.

There is no path around such a lake.
Unlock the spider shed... oars... lifejacket...
A few strokes from shore, the lurch

at page-turn knocks me from the thwart,
my eye missing
the shift to new water.

AN UNEMPLOYED WORKER'S HOME

Morgantown, West Virginia
Walker Evans, July 1935

It's the one in the mirror always sucks up the light,
Gives some back to the real rocker by the newel.
But you know, things in mirrors are always doing backwards.
I can't pin up my hair in front of no mirror—
Just do it by feel, like after dark.

That's what it is—mirrors make everything but them be dark.
And around the edge, where everything tilts there,
It's like looking at two sides of a thing at the same time—
You ever seen a pond with water spiders on top
And you can see the leaves and maybe a turtle down in it?
There's more in mirrors than most folks think—some,
I know some as keeps them covered with a shawl,
Especially at night, you know.
Anyway that rocker's a good one—see how it's tall in the back—
You can lean your head back when you're not working on anything,
Lean your head back and rest it there,
Your elbows on those smooth arms, and the song can just take you.

In winter I move the rocker up close to the fire—
Fire's another thing that mirror takes.
But this is where we keep that rocker in summer.
It gets air and light from the doorway,
And of course you get a headache, too,
When the young'uns come tearing down the staircase.
That's why there's no bowl on that table n'more—
They knocked it right off.

ONE NEED NOT BE A CHAMBER—
TO BE HAUNTED—

Nor does it help to wonder how
or why that airless shadow found
and fell across one's only soul.

No simple shade between the light
and self, it hunts and swallows light—
a greater gravity of darkness.

Nameless dread, the hardest conquered—
at dread my throbbing thumb demands
a thicker pen. Instead of black

I write in daylight blue, though day
is sometimes worse: the fear of night
is human; day is night's best cure.

So when the dark in morning blooms,
or after lunch, or during,
one trembles next to no one, crouched

alone. That very one-ness baits
the beast who looms and shifts,
who thrives by staying free of names.

LATE SUMMER. FLOATING.

The slopes of Mt. Hood birth clouds
one tuft at a time.
They float eastward on the breeze.

Glaciers drip into ravines of dust.
The woods below lie quiet as my heart,
alone on this wide-open lake.

The two of us reach toward each other
across ridges pocked by clear cuts
no matter how close we sit.

The wake of a boat rolls in
year after year
rocking the pebbles back and forth.

Once in a while, a stone
turns all the way over.
The water will carry me.

SO YOU WANT TO GO SPELUNKING

Plan to emerge from the cave at dusk: you'll
find it hard to breathe under the weight of day.

When you see again the hills and trees,
remember the spaces underneath.

Use the toilet while you still have one.

Before entering the cave, stop and sit
until you feel Earth's breath entering sky.

In a cave, no light is bright enough.

It will be a dirty, muddy, hair-messing time.

Earth has no floor.

Darkness is more than the absence of light: it is
what crawls down your neck
when your nose nearly brushes a wall
furry with sleeping bats.

Adrenaline is a powerful antidote to fatigue.

The tightest passages sometimes lead
to the largest rooms.

The promised waterfall may be one you can neither
hear nor shine your headlamp on:
you are at the top; the pool is far below.

Deep in a cave, life distills to one question—
Which way now?

Thick skin will slow the seeping-in
of all the absences you find.

In complete darkness
eyes invent light.

Never forget: rope, water, food, knife, home.

There are no postcards from this country.

2

MUDSICK

The air's been thick as mud,
my legs heavy-weary. My feet

now make sweet mounds under the blanket.
Even uncovered, their pain

would not be visible. They have no
creases deepening between the brows.

Though joints may crack and grate,
the body for the most part suffers mutely

and I've found myself wishing
for the tearlessness of a toe,

an elbow's simple bending
or not. The face

is a complicated thing to organize.
I don't know how people do it.

CROW IN A CROSSWALK

The light turns green. A crow enters the crosswalk
with its head-bobbing bird walk right as a bus
comes hurtling down the block—the crow now
two-legged hopping like a rabbit, like a dog with two
of its feet useless as words in a bilingual dictionary for a
language no one knows. The bus fires street dirt
between black feathers. My tongue,
limp in my mouth. The crow
resumes walking down the sidewalk.

The hopping crow traces a path as jagged as my pulse
on the monitor yesterday—
they had me signing papers
as if sticking a scope down someone's throat
to look at their liver weren't an everyday thing.
Today, it hurts to swallow so I keep thinking I'm sick
but the pictures said—so they tell me—
there is only liver.

In recovery, my heaving sobs felt so good
I went back to the sleep the nurse had given me,
to hold open the door those sobs were coming through.
It was holy, that crying, and tasted of grief.
Iodine stains the IV site.

The light turns green,
autumn 2002. In my dictionary, the season
following summer will never again be fall.
Let the leaves do it. It's their nature,
not mine. Last year what mattered was standing up.
This year driving. Let it rain.
The light turns green. I cross
the intersection. Through the open window
water splatters my black coat.

A JACKHAMMER TAKEN TO MY HEART, MY MIND SETTLES INTO THE CRACKS LIKE DUST

I'm collecting cobwebs—who
builds and leaves these things?—
to make myself a doll house.
I think if my heart has a little
wing-back chair, a good book,
and her feet elevated,
she can lose herself
one beat at a time.

Today the first woman walked in space.
The study, the training, the fears she
conquered, nobody cared about any of it
until the hatch closed behind her.

Astronauts say we live on a jewel,
but they never describe us—
wee devils on a grain of rice.
Is this another kind of running away,
replaying a fourth-grade bike ride,
with her suitcase, across the bridge?
The astronaut said she could see the raging
fires and so she came back.

The chimney's done. Its glued toothpicks
form a tiny stockade. Something very small
stays safe inside. Mom used to help us
upholster empty Morton Salt boxes, cut away
just so, inserting a little cushion
to furnish chairs for a backless living room.

I would've chosen scuba diving.
And I may yet. It's true
you can suffocate either way.
The rhythmic bang of the tank-fillers
reminds me how well
wounds heal in seawater.

Back home I'll fashion gray dust
into her beautiful head
and seat her by the watercolor fireplace.

STORY

I fell down a hole. Not well-
sized, but vaster
than I cared to explore.
The moist space
muffled all sound
so my cries did not echo
but folded in on themselves,
like a road map
or a child's unanswered questions.

It was easy to stay—
never hungry, and warm as August.
I began building
with careful rounds, like a
bricklayer, the sidewalks,
maples, and fleeting cats
of the world I'd fallen from.
I had to imagine sun,
but I still could, adding sunflower
and ripening tomatoes.

It soon began to smell and sound
so like my old neighborhood
that one day I was struck
as I crossed without
looking both ways. I even
have my old job back
and have decided to let
the rains of October fall.

NO DAY LIKE ANY OTHER

The coiled rope in the shed
is a snake, for just a second.

Plates collide, lifting and tearing the fields.

Jam remains in its jar
awaiting a more perfectly toasted slice.

The car has cooled past ticking. The check
in the bank is smaller than it appears.

There is creeping in the dampness
and crawling in the dust—

sounds that keep secrets.

The sky holds gnats, ospreys,
and things with lights that blink in the night.

None of the zippers that broke
were closed. Oil seeps toward shore.

IT WASN'T COURAGE

Later, climbing the stairs
bolted into the cliff,
I met my nine-year-old son.
One look at his face
and I knew that if
I'd had any idea
what a boy might feel
watching his mother
dive off a bridge,
I'd never have done it.

I didn't know why I had to.
New Zealand's south island
is full of brochures. One
stood brighter, spoke
louder than the rest.

For ten days we drove
on the left, against instinct.
Toward distant relations,
along coastlines, down valley,
up tunnel. Burrowing
penguins, glowworm caves.
In Queenstown, finally
I spoke up.

My older son, newly twelve,
came with me onto
the historic bridge.
He was shaking—wind
or fear, it didn't matter—
I sent him back to wait with his dad.

After they wrapped my
ankles in towel and cord,
I had to hop
to the end of a plank
above 150 feet of air
bound by cream-colored
cliffs over a frothing
turquoise river.
They had explanations,
instructions,
cautions,
assurances. I had
a choice: straight down
to enter the water,
outward to avoid it, or
dive the angle in between
and my fingertips
would brush the current
near the tiny yellow raft
that waited.

Then I was springing
into freefall
like in so many dreams,
and the wind caught
in the hood of my coat,
making me spin as I fell.

A bungee recoils
with surprising
gentleness. Up and down
and twirling around
as if gravity had escaped
and canyon-water-sky
was what I breathed.

I flung my arms wide—
to gather in this world
like somersaults on grass—
and let loose a laughter
as big as the gorge.

HEART OF SOAPSTONE

The fir-clad hills of Oregon, clear of
poison ivy and fireflies, have held me so well
that only now, as I begin my unfolding,
do I feel how their bones
bite at my soft places.

A sojourn of twenty-six years, as if
my children drew me to the Northwest
to birth and raise them, and my neck,
which took generations of careful breeding
to get this stiff, turned and complied.

Hope is a thing with talons.
I turn from its grip and look back toward
sweet tea and honeysuckle. I married a man
who didn't understand porch swings. Single now,
needing a job, I think of dogwood and white pine,

and turn back toward the Blue Ridge mountains.
Somewhere, a stream-polished heart
of soapstone tumbles, waiting
for my hand to warm it.

HEADLONG INTO THE ATLANTIC
AFTER TWENTY-SIX YEARS AWAY

The current pulls northward, deepward, and
suddenly my feet find no bottom.
Still the waves invite my dive and rise.
I have to pull and pull always to the south—
arms, legs, a heart just able
to keep my head above water.
I am dancing at the joint
of land and sea and I am no dancer.

To the student of planet Earth,
waveroll and riptide are no mystery.
They've been mapped into equations
that ride the page, rattling shells
in the ears of those who speak the language.
I did, once, and still remember the moment
the chalkboard's Greek showed a standing wave
in fractions and parentheses, clear as any
sun-flecked snapshot.

A boy has rafted beyond the breakers. He rides
and fights the same pull. I kick
at a teenage memory: out about as far as he is,
but no raft. Between me and the beach,
waves spiral with a violence that throws me
further out every try. An hour or more I strive
for shore, my friends surprised at how
I love to swim. I don't have the voice
to reach them, can only keep kicking southward
so as not to lose them, believing I will make it in.

TRIPTYCH

The unstable line
between recollecting pain
and holding a grudge

***

The dam finally broke and floods
the valley clear up to the house where I
watch from a covered porch as whole hillsides
give way and plunge, one after another,
into the clay-brown waves

***

A fork teeters at table's edge
and I'm poised to flinch at its clatter on tile—
sometimes you can see it coming

No straight path
to the center,
these bricks
say turn, turn,
then grant a great sweep
halfway round
this labyrinth's circle.
They turn and turn again,
approaching center
and moving away.
Three hundred and sixty degrees
of perspective.

I returned to
the job market
at forty-five
and learned
motherhood
makes a weak resume.
Five years of steps
to find full-time work.
Three months
to reach layoff.

So I moved away
from the home
I'd painted pumpkin,
wheat, and wine.
Swept my life
onto a truck
and turned
toward a job
across the continent.

LABYRINTH, NEW YEAR

Countless small steps
of settling in
to an apartment
above a wooded ravine
where I pretend
solitude in the suburbs.
Began a career
I'd been aiming for.
It takes everything
I give and returns
almost enough.
The solitude
is real.

Center is the place
you arrive
so as to move away
and know
you will return.

THE MINE TOUR

If I took you on a mine tour, if there were one,
we would get in the cage just before the door
slams shut on the August drought. We'd descend,
trading places with a coal-filled skip whose rise
balances our fall through layers of solid rock
holding water under such pressure that the shaft
must be sealed against it. At the beach, how we used to
love digging holes in wet sand. We had no idea.

We'd see how dim the headlamps are, even in passages
strung with caged lights. The weight of so much rock
thickens the darkness, makes it hard
for light to travel. We'd remember
the mine nearby—its coal seams smolder,
inextinguishable. They no longer use canaries.
To reach the area of active digging, we'd hunch
along a tunnel as low as the one that let

the Pennsylvania miners escape
when the black water broke through.
They raced the flow as it rose past their ankles,
approaching their knees and chins.
Who would we be trusting?
We'd discuss other mines, gold and diamond,
that reach deep, warming toward the core.
Our withdrawals riddle the Earth.

If there were a tour, our headlamps' light
would remind us of light from a lamp to read by.
Outside it would be hot, bright, dry. The city
would want a break from so much sun,
would wish for air conditioning.
And we would know whether down in a mine,
like up here, in a road cut,
the freshly broken rock is the brightest.

AVERSIONS

This time I chose not
to avert my eyes.
The man in blue scrubs
laid out four
collection tubes.
I looked at
the size of them,
looked at my arm,
and decided to watch.
The vein was hard
to find
but gave generously.

I'd been afraid
that watching
would make me
feel faint.
What I felt was
a deep reverberation
when he pulled
the last tube
off the needle:
the force
of a current turned
back on itself.

Not the volume of blood
but its turbulence,
flooding
each tube in turn—
between stoplights, and during
dinner with my son.
The gushing.
The black, black red.

FOURTEEN STORIES ABOVE
A LIGHT RAIL STATION, DENVER

Each time those doors slide shut, as the bells
ding-ding through my hotel room's open window,

I remember: years ago, underneath the airport concourses—
another bell, my children not yet inside the rail car

and I'm sliding into the tunnel away from them,
like the billions of flowers

for a pound of honey and later,
at the edge of my lip, just a trace.

Cruel Atlanta, my younger in the Braves
T-shirt I'd bought him that day.

He's going to enlist, he told me last week.
Why the Army? I ask and ask.

I had yelled *Stay right there!* through the windows
as the tunnel took me.

Each pair of eyes in my car wide, silent,
moving half a step back.

I couldn't know the glass was too thick.
Got off at the very next stop—it took years

to decide whether to jump
the next train back or find a guard.

IEDs, snipers—*Why not the Navy,*
like your Granddad? I was fine

till the guard asked what they were wearing.
And the taller one's brown-haired, the younger

boy blond? she asked, not meeting my eye. My voice
broke while she looked past my shoulder, toward the rails

where those two were getting off a train
like its improbable blossoms and running toward me.

ON "STOKED"

The word must be Anglo-Saxon, with its deeply satisfying
mouthfeel, its Grand-Master-in-the-parade-of-your-life-feel,
in the way that *fucked* is a satisfying oath. *Stoked* may be
less fricative, but its long *o* gloats in a glory *fucked* can only
fantasize about.

And the thing about *stoked* is, when you are, you have no need
to say it because you glow from every pore. Unlike *fucked*,
when you need to declare it over and over again, as if there,
between the *f* and the *u-c-k*, will appear the way out.

But when you're stoked, you want no way out, want to stay
right there in its bonfire—warm, bright, full of promise.

3

IN THE COUNTRY OF THE BONE FLUTE
Bled, Slovenia

It's a strong wind, a clear wind, a give-back-my-breath wind. Blow
my skirt up, ravish me standing. Moan on the mountainsides, slam
all the windows shut, strip bare the plane trees
and frighten the swans.

A wind in the face of which
I'd tuck my beak
under my wing
if I had one.

A thundering bass wind tasting of glacier,
I'm hollow—
I'm hollow—
sing in me.

WALKING BACK TO BETANJA

The sky is white. The rocks
are white. White road, white
horses eating grass.
Buzzing heat and quick lizards.
Mossy rocks with unreadable inscriptions.

Day and night I hear the river
frothing at the mouth of the cave.
This karst swallows rivers whole.
Lakes sink beneath their beds.

Fish with legs and bats, bats, bats—
plenty of fruit and plenty bugs.
A terrier barks at dawn and a cock crows all day.
Vast caverns underlie my bed.
I drown among the stars.

ABOVE THE CAVES OF ŠKOCJAN

A gravel angel speaks
as to a dog
one has loved a long time—
  Always view the light
  from the back
then melds into
the limestone dust.

A man tossing out his garbage
looks up at the sound—
dismisses it as noisy ants.

Atop these hollow hills,
the times I feel small
are like that backside of light.

I climb the steep path
on sturdy legs.
Surely my steps echo
through the chambers underneath.

HOLY GROUND

Betanja, Slovenia

Walking home after midnight, the steep hill
leads past the cemetery
where I pause.
The day held hundreds
of decisions, the wall
between the flowered graves and me
is a good thing.

A hump of dim light on the horizon
lifts my gaze from the candlelit tombstones.
It looks as if the hills are squeezing
an orange egg upward.
It lengthens, grows into a moon
two nights past full. Like a birth
and a cool wet cloth to the neck.

My steps cresting the hill are light
and the abundant stars prickle my skin.
Coming down the other side where the hill
drops off sharply at the inside of the curve,
there, on a broad leaf, something glows
green. I kneel, and through eyes
that have beheld the world
for too many too-bright hours,
I make out a tiny
phosphorescent worm,
just a few millimeters long,
so green and so bright
I sit down. I take off my shoes.

OCEAN CROSSING

from the shade of stem
      to wild rackle of sun and low weed

  between ladder rungs of stalk shade   ant
     makes its many-legged way

daisy ladder   big-headed laughter   sun
     fimbrial petals type their song
        on wind   brick
        of a wall   of a backdrop
                 shadow play
   digitalia

  dirigibles of randy pride
    earth—so it would seem—defying
      lift

    time is the unasked question
    spark the unsought answer

but still the sandlot still the swing and sweat
and bare feet longer each summer
toes   spread wide

BY THE GULF

Waves keep rising
like endless flocks
of starlings
thundering
from trees.

The float,
the fight,
the flattening shoreward.
The pull to the deep,
the lift.

Spume, sticks,
and fragmented
shells dry
in the sun.

A wave reaches
the tip of my foot.
I raise it—

foam
flies on the wind.

SEASCAPE

Shore, rock, gull,
low tide,
and a shutter banging at dusk.

Over all of this spills a blue light.
In the foreground, a figure
takes shape, bending here and there,

keeping an eye on the horizon and the building clouds,
surefooted, as if this landscape
were clothes to relax in at home.

Limpet? Sand dollar? What eyes
seek and fingers touch
is unclear from this distance,

but there will be a tune under the breath.
So much of a day's work
is simply the making of room for hope.

Those weeks of plans falling in on themselves
with great exhalations of disappointment,
of winter, when sunset comes too soon after sunrise—

those are times when the shore—
where the eye can find its limit beyond
the edge of land—is the deepest home.

AGATHA, PIN OAK

Trunk, lobed fingers, your pulse felt not heard:
faerie, from *fata*, goddess of fate—
the inevitable life I might stop believing in
were it not for your night eyes.
Walking this trail in the dark, Agatha,
I know the moment I near your watching,
feel it in the black seed of my brain.
Does your gaze fall thus on all the ones
who pass this way after dusk?

Agatha, tonight my feet will carry me
no further than your broad trunk,
fit to rest my back against.
Low limbs invite my shinny
up into your branches, their ample crook
fit for nestling, for holding this heavy head.
My legs and arms twine around your bark
and I do not fall.
I do not.

LIFT
Koper, Slovenia

FOR NATHAN

At dusk I looked over the dock's rail
and saw among the stones,
under the undulating water, a bunny
trying to get free.
It was too far down for me to reach
and I looked for help.
But then it was only three white stones
there among the rest—
ears, body, tail.

The pilot had to bring down
our small plane in the park—
too wide for the road,
it clipped some trees.
We were thrown around
and as I wondered about the damage
the way cleared.
He was taking off again.

I struggle for air to stay afloat
in the sea of this foreign tongue.
There are those moments we cannot rise
to what we hold within us,
but I wish for you that lift—
the carry, the soar.

TRAVELING EAST

Here, the sun comes to me every morning.
We greet each other with an embrace and he begins
nibbling at my ears, moving down my neck and shoulder
to my spine, the curves of my hip, belly, and breasts and
so begins our day of lovemaking. His fingers slipping over
every inch of my skin, we toss, we tangle, his breath
warm in my hair, between my toes—I take him
places he has never seen and we make
new lands of love, going at it for hours. I soak
up all his juices, sweat them out, the sheets a mess,
until, spent, he must rest at last, so
fades and sinks to sleep.
It is then, only then,
that he comes
to you.

SLIPPERY WORLD

The last time I fell off my blue bike, I found
no reason to get up and brush off.

Bits of sky glowed glorious
between broad leaves
of maple and sycamore.
None of the busy squirrels took notice.

It was good to lie there,
count the varieties of birdsong,
enjoy the orchestration of breezes
chasing the creek down the ravine.

I straightened the bent leg,
tested toes and elbows, but checking
for scrapes, eyeing the wheels—why?
I had hours till sunset.

With each breath, I tasted
life in the air, tried to tease apart
the layered scents—brown leaves,
green ones, hints of honeysuckle...

When the man stopped,
pulling out his phone
before both feet hit the ground,

his brow creased, eyes scanning...
I craned my neck this way and that
to see what could possibly be wrong.

WHY I AM NOT AN EVANGELIST

I bought the vintage Pendleton mancoat
because it could button over my belly and breasts,
and for its flannel pockets—
a godsend when weather demands
a heavy coat.

Lined with satin, it's just as easy
to slip out of as slip into. Its sleeves
are short enough to stay out of my way
and long enough to tuck over gloves,
keeping the chill from the pulse at my wrists.

The wide collar folds up around my cheeks
when it's raw out. In this coat
there is room enough for all of me.
It's heavy, though I don't often notice—it rides
my shoulders or over my arm like no big deal.

And bulky—this woollen coat won't be
simply tossed on a bench or across a chair.
Big as a man it is, and just as hard to ignore.
How could I say to anyone, *This is just the coat for you?*
Most coat racks cannot bear it.

TOM'S CREEK FALLS

From the trailhead—no cars,
no phone signal, no human in earshot—
I'll hike to a waterfall near an old mineshaft

I want to explore. Mica is still mined in these hills.
Pliant sheets spall from boulders
and flakes big as silver dollars litter the trail.

The February sun glints off the lively water
and the mica-bright creek bed, in a double-layered
light that could be blinding, come summer.

The falls are loud, enchanting with a roar
like wind on this quiet afternoon.
The low-angled sun—almost warm—

isolates droplets as they ricochet
off rocks and logs. A moment airborne,
then they're creek again, in water's bewitching way

of being both plural and singular. Water
is said to lie deep in the abandoned mine.
Before I can find its entrance, the torrent's

small breezes, which tickle the leaf meal
and tendrils of late winter life,
strengthen. Is it lowering sun that lifts this wind,

or a change in the weather coming on?
Shadows seep toward my feet. This place
breathes like a fairy grove, even as the shine dims.

No moon will rise tonight, but if the sky stays clear
all this mica will dance with the starlight,
and I do believe I'll find my way home.

Notes

p. 34: The title is from Emily Dickinson.

p. 77: A piece of hollow bone with holes in it, like a flute, was found in a cave in Slovenia. It is thought to be the oldest known musical instrument, though this claim is in dispute.

About the Author

 Kelly Lenox has published poems, prose, translations of poetry and fiction, and book reviews in the U.S. and abroad. Her work has been nominated for a Pushcart Prize and other awards. She is the translator of the chapbook *Chasms* (PM Books: 2003), by the Slovenian poet Barbara Korun. She is co-translator of *Six Slovenian Poets* (UK: Arc, 2006) and *Voice in the Body* (Litterae Slovenicae, 2005).

She lives in Durham, North Carolina, where she is a technical writer and editor for the National Institute of Environmental Health Sciences. She holds an MFA in writing from the Vermont College of Fine Arts, and a BA in environmental science from the University of Virginia.

www.kellylenox.com

About the Artist

Susan Skrzycki received her BFA in dance and choreography from the California Institute of the Arts. She began painting during her 20-year career as a dancer. Self-taught as a visual artist, her pieces include paintings, encaustic, murals, mixed media, and installations.

www.susanskrzycki.com.

About the Designer

Dave Wofford run Horse and Buggy Press in Durham, North Carolina. Twenty years into its run, H&B remains a one person shop and collaborates on a wide scope of printed matter projects, including fine press books printed in house on a hand-fed, hand-cranked letterpress.

www.horseandbuggypress.com

This book was designed in the summer of 2016 by Dave Wofford. The typeface is Dolly, which was designed by Bas Jacobs, Akiem Helmling, Sami Kortemäki and released in 2001.